What Makes a Mammal a Mammal?

A Bucky and Bingo Learning Adventure

Andi Cann

I hope you enjoy learning about mammals today! Please visit my website https://www.andicann.com and register your email address. You will receive a free book and be the first to know about new books, special offers, and free stuff!

If you have a chance, please write a review. It helps other readers and me, an independent author. Thank you!

Andi

A note to parents.

Kids love animals, especially mammals. Perhaps it's because dogs, cats, and other furry creatures are part of our everyday life. Or maybe it's because we humans are mammals. Regardless, there is something special about the diverse world of mammals. From hogs to dogs, from bats to cats, there are many types of mammals. But it can difficult to explain to children how they and their pup are similar.

There are only 5000 types of mammals. Perhaps it's because they are more complex than other creatures. There are between three and nine factors that classify a mammal as a mammal. (Sources disagree!) Some say it is only hair, mammary glands, and middle ear bones that differentiate a mammal from other species. Others include the seven factors listed in this book: warm-blooded, breathe air, born alive, ear bones, large brains, mammary glands, and hair. There are some exceptions to these rules, of course (isn't there always?) But this book will help you explain the similarities between mammals that live in the ocean (like whales) and those who have pouches for their babies (like kangaroos.) Join Bucky and Bingo as they learn about the concept of "animal class" and mammals. Have fun exploring science with your children!

For all parents who support their children's love of reading and animals!

Hi! I'm Bucky. This is Bingo. Bingo and I were talking. He thinks that I am an animal. Say what?

I'm a human, not an animal. I know **HE** is an animal. But, come to think of it, I'm not sure what kind of animal he is, besides a dog, of course!

We decided to consult the book.

The book says that dogs are mammals. Then, it said that dolphins are also mammals. What? Dogs and dolphins are both

mammals? How can that be?
Dolphins live in water. Dogs live on land.   I don't get it.

The book says an elephant is a mammal, as is a bat! The elephant is HUGE, and the bat is super tiny. Size must not matter if you are a mammal.

Look! The elephant is huge compared to the mouse on its trunk.

The book said that mammals are mammals if they have the five "B's" plus hair and milk. Huh? What does that mean?

We read a little bit more. For a mammal to be a mammal, it must breathe air. Okay! This bear breathes air. It must be a mammal!

The next "B" is the brain. Mammals have BIG brains! This little fox has a big brain, especially compared to this tiny bird!

The next "B" is blood. Mammals have warm blood. That sounds gross, but it just means that when the air is cold, mammals are warm! Even this very furry polar bear who lives in the snow stays warm!

Mammals grow inside their mother and are born alive, like this baby horse! The next "B" is birth!

The last "B" is bone. Mammals have middle ear bones. Those are the bones that help us hear. Mammals also have backbones from head to rear!

Two more things that make a mammal a mammal — hair, and milk. Wait, what?

Mammals are mammals if they have hair (or fur, that is)!

And, when they're babies, they drink milk!

Mammals are mammals because they have hair.

Mammals, just mammals, are born breathing and bare.

Mammals have big brains, warm blood, and bony ears and backs.

Mammals drink milk for meals and snacks.

So, now that we know all about mammals let's take a look at this new animal. What do you think? Is a camel a mammal?

Does she have the five "B's?" Warm blood, check! Big brain, ear and backbone, breathing air, check, check, check. It is born live and drinks milk. A camel is a mammal!

Here's an ostrich. Is it a mammal? Nope, an ostrich has feathers. It's a bird! Remember, a bird is a bird because it has feathers!

What about this bat? It flies like a bird. But, it has hair! And, it's warm-

blooded, born alive, breathes air, and has ear and backbones. Yep, a bat is a mammal!

Hi, I'm a penguin! Am I a mammal? I don't fly and live with the polar bears. But I'm a bird. My babies are hatched from eggs not born alive!

What about this bunny? I see a lot of hair.

A bunny, a beaver, a fox, and a zebra. They are all mammals if you pleasa!

And... humans are mammals, too! That's right, you! YOU are a mammal, Woo hoo!

It's hard to believe that you are in the same animal class as sheep and goats, but you are a mammal just like a horse, of course!

Bingo, today we learned a mammal is a mammal because it has hair. Mammals are mammals because they breathe air.

Mammals are mammals because of warm blood, ear and backbones. They have big brains and are born alive. They drink milk and sometimes, they even fly!

Wasn't it fun learning about mammals, today?

Mammals are cool and are a part of our lives every day.

Bucky and Bingo and I would like to say,

Thanks for joining our adventure and play!

Mammals, in order of appearance:

Front Cover: Goat

Page 7 Golden Retriever and Labrador Retriever Dogs

Page 8 Dolphin

Page 9 Bat (specify)

Page 10 African Elephant and Mouse

Page 11 Giraffe

Page 12 Brown Bear

Page 13 Baby Red Fox and Cockatiel

Page 14 Baby Polar Bear

Page 15 Horses

Page 16 Baby Pig

Page 17 Hedgehog

Page 18 Orangutan

Page 19 Mother and Baby Cow

Page 20 Hamster

Page 21 Camel

Page 23 Ostrich

Page 24 Grey, Long-eared Bat

Page 25 Penguin

Page 26 Rabbit

Page 27 Zebra, Horse

Page 28 Human Baby

Page 29 Pygmy Goat, Horse

Page 30 Hamster

Page 31 Sugar Glider (Flying squirrel)

Page 32 Dog

Back Cover: Koalas

This book is a work of fiction. Names, characters, businesses, places, events, locales, and incidents are either the products of the author's imagination or used in a fictitious manner. Any resemblance to actual persons, living or dead, or actual events is purely coincidental.

We welcome you to include brief quotations in a review. If you would like to reproduce, store, or transmit the publication in whole or in part, please obtain written permission from the publisher. Otherwise, please do not store this publication in a retrieval system. Please do not transmit in any form or by any means electronic, mechanical, printing, photocopying, recording, or otherwise. Please honor our copyright! For permissions: Contact MindView Press via email: mindviewpress@gmail.com

Published by MindView Press: Hibou

ISBN-13:   978-1-949761-17-7   eBook

ISBN-13:   978-1-949761-18-4   Paperback

Copyright©2018 by Andrea L. Kamenca. All rights reserved.

Other books by Andi Cann in the Animal Class series:

What makes a bird a bird?

ANDI CANN

What makes a bug a bug?

ANDI CANN

www.ingramcontent.com/pod-product-compliance
Lightning Source LLC
Chambersburg PA
CBHW040224040426
42333CB00051B/3445